MOSES 1

KEPT ʙʏ GOD

BOOK 1 (TOLD FROM EXODUS 1–2)

CARINE MACKENZIE
Illustrated by
Graham Kennedy

© Copyright Carine Mackenzie 2008
Published by Christian Focus Publications,
Geanies House, Fearn, Tain, Ross-shire, IV20 1TW, Scotland, U.K.
www.christianfocus.com
Printed in China

Amram and Jochebed lived with their children Miriam and Aaron in the land of Egypt. Their family had moved there many years before when Joseph was prime minister.

At first Pharaoh, the King, treated them well. But after Joseph died, another Pharaoh made them all slaves. Amram and the other men had the back-breaking work of making bricks, or working in the fields.

Pharaoh was the ruler of Egypt and a very cruel man. He ordered that all baby boys born to Hebrew families should be killed at birth.

However the
nurses who helped
the mothers when
the babies were born,
refused to obey him. God
was pleased with them.
But then Pharaoh ordered
that the baby boys should be
thrown into the River Nile.

A baby son was born to Amram and Jochebed – a little brother for Miriam and Aaron. The family had to be very careful to keep the new baby hidden.

After three months it became more and more difficult to hide him in the house, without the Egyptian people knowing he was there.

Jochebed thought of a clever plan to save her baby boy. She made a cradle of bulrushes and coated it with tar to make it waterproof. She carefully placed him in the basket which floated gently at the edge of the River Nile among the reeds.

Miriam watched from a distance to see what would happen.

Pharaoh's daughter, the princess, came down to bathe in the river. She noticed the basket among the reeds.

"Bring that basket to me," she ordered her servant.

The baby began to cry when the basket was opened. The princess felt sorry for the little baby.

"This must be one of the Hebrew children,"
the princess said.

Miriam came out of hiding
to speak to the princess.

"Shall I go and get one of
the Hebrew women to nurse the baby
for you?" she asked.

"Yes, go," replied the princess.
Miriam ran to fetch her mother.

"Look after this child," the princess told Jochebed, "and I will pay you wages."

The baby's life was saved and he was now back with his family. God was looking after him.

God looks after us every day of our lives.

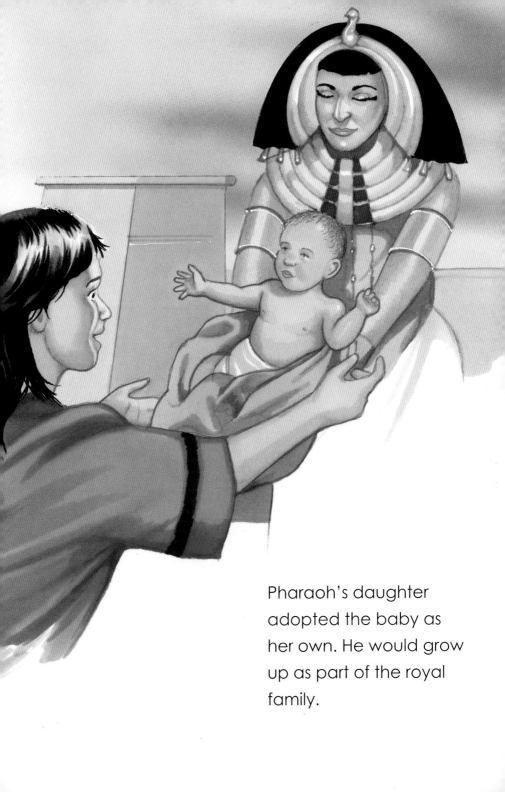

Pharaoh's daughter adopted the baby as her own. He would grow up as part of the royal family.

She gave him the name Moses which means "drawn out" because he was drawn out of the water when he was found in the basket.

But his real mother was able to look after him free from worry and danger. His parents would have taught him about the Lord God.

We need to learn the teaching from the Bible too.

When Moses grew older he went
to live at the royal palace where
he was educated like a prince.
But he never forgot that he
was a Hebrew and he always
worshipped the one true God.

God never changes. He still wants us
to worship him.

Moses was sad to see the Hebrew people, his people, slaving for their Egyptian masters. One day Moses saw an Egyptian beating a slave. This made him very angry.

He killed the Egyptian and buried the body in the sand when no one was looking.

The next day he came across two
Hebrew men fighting. When he tried
to stop them, one man said to him,
"Do you mean to kill me, as you
killed the Egyptian?"

Moses was scared. It was no secret that he had killed an Egyptian. Pharaoh was furious when he heard. He wanted to kill Moses but he escaped to the country of Midian.

God kept Moses safe through dangerous times. He was spared as a baby from death. He was kept in his family where he learned the ways of God. He was given a good home and schooling in Pharaoh's palace. God was in control of all the events of Moses' life.

Moses was glad to belong to the people of God. It is important for us to belong to the family of God by believing in the Lord Jesus Christ.